9

EVERYTHING YOU NEED TO KNOW WHEN YOU ARE

NEW YORK TIMES BESTSELLING AUTHOR

KIRSTEN MILLER

ILLUSTRATED BY ELLEN DUDA

AMULET BOOKS • NEW YORK

Library of Congress Cataloging-in-Publication Data
Names: Miller, Kirsten, 1973– author.
Title: Everything you need to know when you are 9 / by Kirsten Miller.
Description: New York: Amulet Books, 2020. | Summary: Advises the reader on many
aspects of being nine, from how to handle ghosts and monsters to how to help
someone who is choking.
Identifiers: LCCN 2019033769 (print) | LCCN 2019033770 (ebook) |
ISBN 9781419742323 (hardcover) | ISBN 9781683357803 (ebook)
Subjects: CYAC: Life skills—Fiction. | Interpersonal relations—Fiction. |
Etiquette—Fiction. | Humorous stories.
Classification: LCC PZ7.M6223 Eve 2020 (print) | LCC PZ7.M6223 (ebook) | DDC [Fic]—dc23
LC record available at https://lccn.loc.gov/2019033769
LC ebook record available at https://lccn.loc.gov/2019033770

Printed and bound in China
10 9 8 7 6 5 4

Amulet Books are available at special discounts when purchased in quantity
for premiums and promotions as well as fundraising or educational use.
Special editions can also be created to specification.
For details, contact specialsales@abramsbooks.com or the address below.

Amulet Books® is a registered trademark of Harry N. Abrams, Inc.

ABRAMS The Art of Books
195 Broadway, New York, NY 10007
abramsbooks.com

FOR GEORGIA AND HER COUSINS ZOE, ROWAN, RILEY, AND RHYS—
THE COOLEST, CRAZIEST, AND MOST DELIGHTFULLY
DISGUSTING KIDS I'VE EVER HAD THE PLEASURE TO KNOW

THiS iS A BOOK FOR EVERYONE TURNiNG

9

9 IS AN AWESOME AGE. ONE OF THE BEST.

Some say it's even better than 8!
(Please don't tell any 8-year-olds.) You should enjoy every second of the next 365 days. You're going to learn a great deal this year, but there are a few things they won't teach you in school. That's why I wrote this book—so you'll know everything I wish someone had told me back when I was your age. Some of the stuff is serious. Some of it's gross. And some of it will make other parents question my sanity. But I'm going to tell you anyway.

IS IT OK TO LOOK AT MY POOP?

Not only is it okay, it's a sign that you're well on your way to being a doctor! You only have 22 years of school left to go!

Poop can tell you a lot about your body. How? Think of it this way—the human body is a machine. What that machine makes is poop. If what your body is producing doesn't look right, or feel right, or smell right (yeah, I said it), you might need to make a few simple repairs to your machine.

Weird poop is usually no big deal. If you're not quite sure what to do, don't be afraid to show someone. (Try a parent. This isn't the best way to make friends.) Tell your parents it's all part of your medical training. They'll be so proud.

HARD POOP

If your poop is hard and difficult to push, drink more water and eat lots of fruits and vegetables. (This isn't a trick to get you to eat healthy—it really works.) Your poop should be feeling better in no time. If not, try a few prunes. They taste a lot better than they look.

SOFT POOP

If it's diarrhea you have, you've probably already sounded the alarm. (If not, go do it now.) If your poop's just a little too soft, try eating foods like bananas, rice, apples, or toast until you're back to normal.

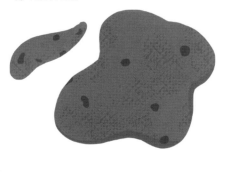

GREEN POOP

Let me guess—either you really love salad or someone's been making you eat a whole lot of kale. Green vegetables are usually responsible for green poop. Sometimes medicine can cause green poop, too. Here's the rule when it comes to green poop—once is nothing to worry about and twice is no big deal. Three in a row, however, is a fascinating mystery that you'll want to solve. Get your mom, dad, or most beloved adult to help.

RED POOP

Nothing's weirder than a red poop in the toilet. Before you freak out, think back to your last few meals. Were beets involved? Any stewed tomatoes? If so, there's your answer. (Happens to all of us.) If not, follow the instructions for black poop.

BLACK POOP

If your poop is black—I mean really black, not just dark brown—it's time to get your parents on the case. Black poop can be caused by all sorts of things (like vitamins). But don't keep this one a secret, and if you end up going to see a doctor, don't worry. Doctors love talking about poop.

RAINBOW POOP

Congratulations, you're a unicorn. (Or you need to stop eating crayons.)

WHAT TO DO iF SOMEONE CAN'T STAND YOU

IT MAKES NO DiFFERENCE HOW WONDERFUL YOU ARE. THERE ARE gOiNg TO BE PEOPLE WHO DON'T LIKE YOU.

I know! It makes no sense! You're fun and interesting and you bathe regularly. Everyone should love you. I totally agree! But that's not how the world works.

Now that we've gotten the bad news out of the way, here's the good news. There are billions of people in the world. Some of them won't want to be friends with you. Maybe they won't like your haircut. Maybe you'll remind them of a cousin who pinches them. It doesn't matter why, because . . . WHO CARES? If you're as awesome as we both know you are, plenty of people out there are going to recognize it.

So, if you meet someone who isn't nice or gives you the cold shoulder, here's what to do:

DON'T DO ANYTHING

Don't try to win them over. Don't try to be who they want you to be. Just be yourself and find friends who like you for who you are.

GET A MOVE ON

There are people out there who would love to meet someone just like you. But don't sit around waiting for them to knock on your door. Friends are a lot like buried treasure: You're never going to find them unless you start looking!

WHAT TO DO iF YOU SEE A GHOST

I lived with a ghost for 4 whole years. It turned out to be a wonderful—and educational—experience!

REMEMBER: GHOSTS AREN'T ALL BAD

Ghosts are like people. (Probably because they used to BE people.) Some are good and some are rotten. So, don't go running and screaming the second you see, hear, or smell a ghost. There's a very good chance that it's friendly—and friendly ghosts are very handy to have around.

DO SOME RESEARCH

The best way to make friends with your ghost is to get to know him/her/it. Find out who lived in your house before you moved in. (Or who might be buried beneath it.) Even if your ghost isn't the friendliest spirit, your research may help you understand why they do what they do. (And help you make sure someone else ends up with the ghost's favorite bedroom!)

HAVE A CHAT

If your ghost isn't nasty, don't be afraid to talk to it. (Just don't expect it to talk back!) Let it know that you're happy to share your house—as long as it promises there will be NO SURPRISES. You don't want your ghost showing up in the bathroom mirror while you're brushing your teeth—or tapping you on the shoulder while you're heading downstairs to the cellar. (You don't need a Ouija board to chat to your ghost. Just wait until the house is empty of other humans and speak out loud!)

GATHER EVIDENCE

The biggest problem with having a ghost is that most living people refuse to believe you. So, grab your camera and start taking pictures whenever you sense that your ghost is around. You never know what will turn up in the photos!

9

WHAT TO DO iF YOU FAiL

I'm sorry to break this to you, but you are not going to be good at everything you try to do. In fact, you're going to be terrible at many, many things.

YOU WILL FAIL IMPORTANT TESTS.

LOSE BIG GAMES.

STINK AT KARAOKE.

WRITE HORRIBLE ESSAYS.

BREAK EXPENSIVE STUFF.

DROP PHONES IN THE TOILET.

INVENT THINGS THAT DON'T WORK.

Sounds terrible, right?
Why don't we take a moment to feel
bad about all of that?

Done? Good.

Everybody fails.

Over and over and over again. But you can choose what kind of failure you want to be. Here are your options:

A. You can be the sort of kid who crawls into bed and spends the afternoon weeping,

OR

B. You can the kind of person who sees failure as a challenge and gets mad.

That's right. Get mad. Be angry at yourself. At the people who tell you you can't do something. At the manufacturers of cheap karaoke equipment that makes your voice sound awful. As soon as you get that fire burning in your belly, go out and prove everyone wrong. Try harder. Practice more. Spend time figuring it all out. The truth is, you'll probably keep on failing. Over and over and over again. Until one day . . . you start kicking some serious butt.

You see, failing can be great if you don't let it stop you! If it makes you work harder and keep trying, failing can be the first step to success!

SO, WHAT'S IN SNOT ANYWAYS?

And what happens if I get some in my mouth?
(By accident, of course.)

When you were 8, you learned how to make lovely fake boogers. (Ah, that was fun, wasn't it?) **Now that you're a year older, it's time for you to know all about the real stuff.**

SNOT IS A DELIGHTFUL SUBSTANCE OTHERWISE KNOWN AS MUCUS.

Lots of different parts of your body make mucus, but nose mucus (aka: snot, boogers, nose oysters, etc.) is by far the most famous.

Your nose makes a surprising amount of snot every day. (I've heard as much as a liter!) It's there to trap bad things like bacteria or viruses before they can make their way up your nose and into the rest of your body.

So, it's pretty good stuff!
You should be glad that you have it!

BUT LET'S GET TO THE MOST IMPORTANT POINT . . .
IS IT EDIBLE?

Snot is mostly water with a little sugar, salt, and protein thrown in. (Boogers form when the water starts to dry up.) It's probably healthier than a lot of the junk food you eat—and it's definitely not going to kill you if you "accidentally" get some in your mouth. (You swallow most of the snot you make anyway.) However, it is my duty to inform you that other people will be SUPER grossed out if they see you eating snot. **If you ever get the urge to give it a taste, do so when no one is looking.**

HOWEVER, IF YOUR SNOT HAPPENS TO BE YELLOW OR GREEN, THAT'S A SIGN THAT IT'S FILLED WITH BACTERIA. The only place for colorful snot is a tissue. (If you don't have a tissue, use a scrap of paper or a gum wrapper. Under no circumstances should you wipe your snot on a wall!) **Make sure to wash your hands after blowing your nose!** And avoid other people's snot whenever possible, no matter what beautiful color it happens to be.

HOW TO DEAL WITH STRANGERS

When I was a kid, my parents would tell me,

"DON'T TALK TO STRANGERS!"

It always struck me as a weird thing to say.

After all, we have to talk to lots of strangers every day. I don't know the man behind the counter at the grocery store, but if he says "hello" to me, it's probably not a good idea to scream and run away. Right?

The truth is, adults warn kids about "strangers" because there are some really bad people in the world, and you need to avoid them. It's not that hard if you know what you're doing. But how are you supposed to deal with strangers if you're not really sure what one is, or which ones are bad?

Here's how I think of it. Someone is a stranger if:

1.
You don't know their first AND last name. (Mr. or Ms. don't count as first names.)

AND

2.
They are more than 3 years older than you. (Speak to all the strange 9-year-olds you want.)

So, what's the deal with strangers? When should you talk to them—and when should you walk away?

WHEN A STRANGER SAYS HI

Go ahead and say hi. That never hurt anyone.

WHEN A STRANGER WANTS TO SAY MORE THAN HI

If you're with your parents or another adult, go ahead and chat. If you're by yourself, don't stop. Keep on moving.

WHEN A STRANGER TOUCHES YOUR HEAD, ARMS, OR BACK

If your parents aren't with you, this is a problem. If someone you don't know touches you, you should say STOP at the top of your lungs. If they don't stop when you tell them to, follow the instructions in the next box.

WHEN A STRANGER GRABS YOU OR TOUCHES YOU ANYWHERE ELSE

OK, you now have permission to go completely nuts. Scream, kick, punch, bite. Seriously. Make them wish they had never messed with you. Do anything you can to break free and draw attention. And as soon as you're able, RUN.

A STRANGER OFFERS YOU A RIDE

Never, ever get in ANYONE'S car unless one of your parents knows where you are and has TOLD you in advance that it's OK.

I'm sure this all sounds pretty scary, and it is. But now you know what to do, and that knowledge makes you a whole lot safer!

WHY CAN'T i CHAT WITH PEOPLE ONLINE ?!

Let's go back to strangers for the moment.
Remember the rule about not talking to people you
don't know when your parents aren't around?
Yeah, well that goes for the Internet too.

Even if someone gives you their first and last name.
Even if they claim they're 9 years old, too—you shouldn't
talk to them online. Why? Because you can't see people
online—so you have no idea if they're telling the truth.

SOMETIMES PEOPLE USE THE INTERNET TO PRETEND TO BE THINGS THEY'RE NOT—

like kids or girls or famous celebrities. The people who
do this are up to no good. If you end up talking to them,
they could say things you don't want to hear—or show
you things you don't want to see. So, it's smart to avoid
talking to strangers online. And since pretty much
everyone on the internet is a stranger, it's a good idea
to save your conversations for real life.

HOW TO TELL A GOOD JOKE

Along with being interesting, being funny is one of the very best things you can be.

Some people are born funny. They can make you pee your pants laughing every time they open their mouths. But most of us have to teach ourselves how to tell jokes. Fortunately, it's really not that hard if you follow these rules.

HAVE FUN!

Choose a joke that YOU think is incredibly funny. Then practice your joke a few times so that you're totally prepared and relaxed when you find the right moment to tell it.

CHOOSE THE PERFECT AUDIENCE

If your joke is about your grandmother's enormous cat, Jabba, your friends who've never met her cat might not understand what's so funny. So, save the joke for your aunts, uncles, and cousins. They'll probably fall off their chairs laughing.

MAKE SURE YOUR PUNCH LINE IS A BIG SURPRISE

Every great joke has a twist at the end—something your audience won't see coming. The more you surprise people, the harder they'll laugh.

HAM IT UP

Don't be afraid to use different voices or make funny faces. If you're already funny looking, use it to your advantage!

LAUGH

You should always laugh at your own jokes! (If you don't find a joke funny, you shouldn't be telling it.) Laughing is contagious—and if you laugh your butt off, your audience will probably crack up, too.

DON'T MAKE FUN OF THINGS PEOPLE CAN'T HELP

It's lazy and mean. For example, never tell jokes about the way someone looks. But if that someone's a bully, feel free to tell all the jerk jokes you like.

WHAT TO DO WHEN YOU MEET SOMEONE "DIFFERENT"

THIS ONE IS SUPER EASY.
TREAT HIM OR HER THE WAY YOU WOULD
WANT TO BE TREATED.

But let's talk about the word "different" for a moment. What does it mean? We often say people are "different" when they're not **EXACTLY** like us. Maybe they believe other things. Or they have hair or skin that's not the same shade as ours. Or perhaps their bodies don't function just like yours or mine.

Differences like these can seem huge at times. But they're not. All human beings are MUCH MORE similar than we are different. Our bodies are all filled with the same kinds of blood. We all go to the bathroom (though our toilets can be *very different*). We love our families. And we all need friends.

I finished with friends for a reason. You need friends, too, right? When we're kids, we often end up hanging out with people who are similar to us. But here's the secret:

You will grow up to be a FAR more interesting human being if you make an effort to know people who are different. Not only will you learn much more about the world, you'll never be lonely wherever you go.

27

WHAT TO DO iF YOU GET LOST

If you have a phone, this shouldn't be a huge problem. But you're 9, so you might not have a phone yet. If you do, you're probably too lucky to get lost anyway.

If you're one of the millions of phoneless 9-year-olds out there, the answer to this question depends a great deal on **WHERE** you're lost. It also depends on whether you've memorized your home address and your parents' phone numbers by now. (If you haven't, go do it this instant! This was on the list of things to do before you turn 9! Stop reading and get to work!)

OK, done? Now here's what to do.

IF YOU'RE LOST IN THE WOODS

1. I hope you told someone where you were going. ALWAYS do this. It's a lot easier to search for someone who's lost in the woods than it is to search for someone who could be anywhere on PLANET EARTH.

2. Next, when you realize you're lost, STOP MOVING. If people are looking for you, they're more likely to find you if you stay in one place. If you know how to SAFELY build a fire, do it. If not, join the Boy Scouts or Girl Scouts as soon as possible—or have a parent teach you. A fire will not only keep you warm if you're stuck for a while, the smoke will rise into the sky and help people locate you.

There's obviously a lot more you can learn. Knowing how to build a shelter, for example, would come in handy. So, if you plan to spend a lot of time in the woods, get a book of survival skills and study it!

IF YOU'RE LOST IN A CITY, TOWN, OR STORE

If you know your parents' phone numbers, this one is easy.

JUST LOOK FOR SOMEONE WHO LOOKS NICE AND HAS LITTLE KIDS.

Mothers of babies and/or toddlers are best. (Why? People with little kids generally don't have the time or the energy to mess with other people's children.) **When you find a person who matches this description, ask to borrow her phone to call your parents.** She will almost certainly let you. (If she won't, she's not the kind of person you should be dealing with anyway.)

If you DON'T know your parents' phone numbers, GO LEARN THEM RIGHT NOW. If you manage to get lost before you can recite them by heart, follow the instructions above. Tell the person what the situation is and ask for their help. If they don't know how to help, suggest they escort you to a police station. **DON'T BE ASHAMED TO CRY.** Crying is an excellent way to encourage adults to help you.

IF YOU'RE LOST AT SEA

I'm really not the best person to be giving advice on this subject. But I do hope you're not going out to sea on your own yet. Leave that for when you're ten. (Just kidding.) However, if you think there's a chance that you might get lost at sea, please consult a salty old mariner or a pirate and ask him or her to teach you how to fish with your hands, collect rainwater, and navigate by the stars.

IF YOU'RE LOST IN LIFE

We all get lost in life sometimes, though 9 IS a bit young to be feeling this way. (But hey, I'm not judging! I know it's tough being a kid.) Here's what I recommend:

FIND SOMETHING YOU REALLY LOVE AND THROW YOURSELF INTO IT.

Maybe it's sports. Maybe it's knitting. Maybe it's proving that Bigfoot is real. It doesn't really matter what it is—as long as you love it. Read everything you can find on the subject. Practice as often as possible. **Being passionate about something will make you feel great—and help you find the path you want to take!** (PS: This advice works for people of all ages!)

HOW TO CRY ON CUE

This is a skill that can really come in handy. What other trick can win you an Oscar, get your butt out of hot water, and impress your friends? So how do you do it?

DON'T BE AFRAID TO CRY

I don't care who you are or how tough you may be—when bad stuff happens, there's nothing wrong with a good cry. It doesn't make you weak. It makes you a human being.

DRINK LOTS OF WATER

Need to burst into tears at just the right moment? Chug a bottle of water beforehand. You can't turn on the waterworks if your body's too dry.

IMAGINE SOMETHING THAT MAKES YOU SAD

Maybe nothing terrible has ever happened to you. (Lucky you!) No worries. That's what Pixar movies are for. Every one of them has a scene designed to make you blubber like a baby. *Toy Story*, *Up*, *Finding Nemo*—I've cried at all of them. Go watch a few and find the scene that works best for you.

PRACTICE, PRACTICE, PRACTICE

What—you think this is something you can get right the first time you try it? Nope. Like everything else, you're going to have to practice if you want to get good.

FIND AN ONION—PREFERABLY A YELLOW ONE

This works like a charm. Unfortunately, onions are super smelly and aren't always available when you really need them.

DON'T FORCE IT AND DON'T OVERDO IT

If you try too hard, the crying will look fake. If you can't manage to squeeze out the tears, settle for just looking really sad. And don't use this trick too often (unless it's for entertainment purposes). If you do, people will just find you annoying.

WHAT TO DO iF YOU'RE HUNGRY

At the age of 9, you're perfectly able to make yourself a meal. I know, know—it's nice having adults do all the work. Luckily for you, they'll probably continue to do most of the cooking for a few years to come. But you shouldn't need to bug someone else every time you get hungry.

Not allowed use the stove yet, you say? No worries, my friend. You don't need a pan or a burner to make the best food on earth. I'm talking about the magnificent **SANDWICH.** There are a million different kinds of sandwiches. Some require years of training and several advanced degrees if you want to prepare them properly. But here are a few that require little more than 2 pieces of bread, a few utensils, and stuff to shove inside.

PEANUT BUTTER, HONEY, AND BANANA

The PB&J is the classic sandwich. If you don't know how to make that one, you have bigger problems than an empty stomach. (Hint: peanut butter AND jelly are involved.) But I prefer the PBH&B. Take a big spoonful of peanut butter and mix it with a small spoonful of honey until it's nice and smooth. Then use a butter knife to cut a banana into thin slices. Smear a piece of bread with the peanut butter and honey. Add the banana slices and then another piece of bread on top of it all. The PBH&B isn't exactly health food, but it's darn good eating.

TUNA FISH

This is another super easy one. Dump a can of tuna into a bowl. Mix in a big spoonful of mayonnaise. If you like your sandwiches nice and bland, this should be enough, but I use 3 secret ingredients when I make mine. The first 2 are salt and pepper (which most people never even think about), but the third is the most important: pickles. Cut them into slices or little cubes with a butter knife and mix them right in.

CREAM CHEESE AND CUCUMBER

It doesn't sound all that great, but I promise it's awesome. Smear a piece of bread with cream cheese. Add thin cucumber slices and a little salt and pepper. When you're done, don't forget the most important part: Use a butter knife to cut off the crusts. Then cut each sandwich into 3 smaller finger sandwiches. I promise it makes all the difference.

MEAT AND CHEESE

It really doesn't matter what kind of sliced meat you use—or what kind of sliced cheese. It's all going to taste pretty good together. The hard part is choosing the right extras. Pretty much anything can go on a sandwich. It just depends on what you like! I love to put lots of onions and lettuce on my sandwiches. But I'd never touch a tomato. Sometimes I even add potato chips for the crunch. So, go through your fridge and figure out what might taste good to you. If you come up with a combination that you love—and that grosses everyone else out—you've found your PERFECT sandwich.

CAN I EAT iT?

You've just gotten home from school and you're rooting through the refrigerator, looking for things to put on a sandwich. You're so hungry that almost everything looks *amazing*. But if your refrigerator is anything like mine, there are hidden dangers lurking inside. Pick the wrong Tupperware dish, and you could end up spending the night in the bathroom.

So, before you dig in, ask yourself the following questions:

DO YOU KNOW WHAT IT IS?

This is *not* the time to try something new. If you don't recognize it—and there's no one around who knows what it is—*don't eat it!* People stick all kinds of crazy stuff in their fridges. It could be your dad's latest gourmet delight. Or it could be a slug habitat for your sister's science experiment. You just don't know!

IS IT OLDER THAN YOU?

Many foods have their expiration date written right on the package. That's the day when the food may no longer be good. Every fridge in the country is filled with food that's WAY older than it should be. If you're ever bored, have a look in the fridge. There's probably at least one thing in there that's as old as you are!

HOW MUCH DOES IT STINK?

Sure, it looks fine. But how does it smell? You have a nose for a reason—it helps you tell when good food's begun to go rotten. Use it! If your afternoon snack reeks of bad body odor, dead things, smelly feet, or farts, don't put it anywhere near your mouth.

WILL EATING IT ENDANGER YOUR LIFE?

There's a big, delicious piece of cake sitting right there on the second shelf. Your mouth starts watering. Your belly is rumbling. But think hard before you take a bite! That cake could belong to someone else. Is it worth starting a family war over? (Who knows—maybe it is. I just want you to be prepared.)

DOES IT HAVE FUR?

Does the food have any mold on it? What about slime? Has it turned a color you rarely see in nature? Does it look like it could get up and walk off the plate? These are definitely signs that you want to avoid it.

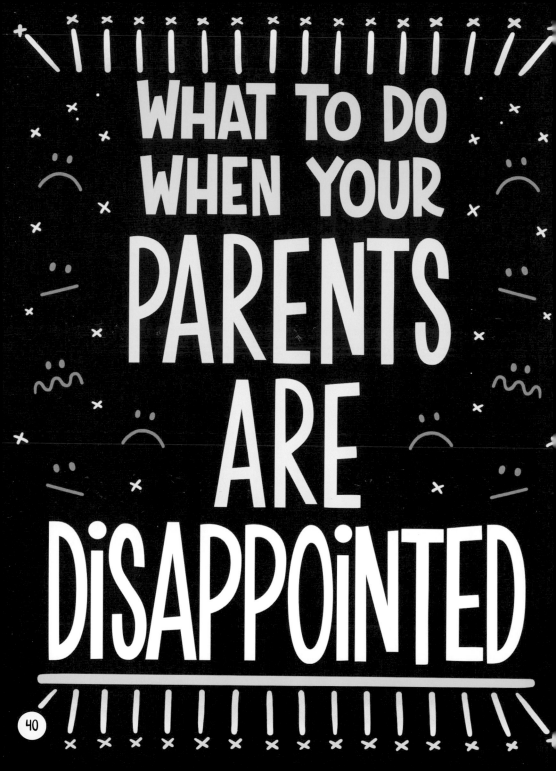

WHAT TO DO WHEN YOUR PARENTS ARE DISAPPOINTED

FIRST OF ALL, IT'S IMPORTANT TO REALIZE THAT YOU'RE NOT ALONE.
CHILDREN HAVE BEEN "DISAPPOINTING" PARENTS SINCE THE BEGINNING OF TIME.

I'd say it's not a big deal, but I don't know that for sure. **Most parents only pull out the disappointed card when you've done something pretty bad.** When it happens to you, it can seem like the end of the world. It isn't, of course. I disappointed my parents quite a few times growing up, and yet I grew up to be a decent human being who's never gone to jail and happens to give excellent advice.

The truth is, having parents who are disappointed isn't such a terrible thing. **It means they believe in you—and they think you can do better.** Parents are usually your biggest fans, and they want you to do well whenever you're able. If they didn't believe you could do it, they wouldn't waste their time being disappointed. They'd spend it taking long, luxurious baths. Don't believe me? Just ask them.

SO, HERE'S WHAT TO DO iF YOUR PARENTS ARE DiSAPPOINTED.

Your mom and/or dad may be angry/sad/slightly nauseous for a while, but there is a way to win them back over. **You see, all parents have a secret weakness.** We all want to believe that we're really great at our jobs. First, tell them you were listening and you want to do better. After that, really give it a go. Do your best to improve. Ignore your annoying siblings. Resist the urge to paint the living room purple. Don't feed the dog Cheetos. You can do better! We all believe in you!

YOU'LL NEVER BE PERFECT (NO ONE iS)

BUT JUST PUTTiNG iN SOME EFFORT WiLL MAKE YOUR PARENTS FEEL PROUD. OF YOU—AND THEMSELVES.

HOW TO SAY YOU'RE SORRY

HEY, YOU!!!

I know "How to Make Fake Poop" is a lot more fun, but don't skip ahead! This one's important! There's a very good chance you've been saying you're sorry the wrong way. And saying it right is definitely something you should know how to do at your age!

Whew! I'm so glad you decided to read this. Because you're going to screw up millions of times in your life. In fact, I'd be willing to bet you're going to do it again today. You could mush someone's toes with the heel of your shoe. You could (accidentally) insult your brother's new hairdo. You might even break your dad's favorite teacup. You're going to have to say sorry, of course. **I hope you know how, because the wrong kind of sorry could make everything worse.**

FIRST YOU HAVE TO SAY IT

It's really easy. Just start with this: "I'm sorry." You'd be surprised how often people forget those 2 little words. A good apology can't begin any other way. And when you're choosing your third word, make sure it's not BUT. This is no time for excuses!

ADMIT YOU DID SOMETHING WRONG

After you say "I'm sorry," the next word should be FOR. At this point, you have to admit what you did. It should go a little something like this . . . "I'm sorry for painting the living room purple." Or "I'm sorry for hiding all of your socks."

UNDERSTAND HOW THEY FEEL— AND TRY TO MAKE THEM FEEL BETTER

Put yourself in the other person's shoes. Why are they so upset? Let them know you understand how you've made them feel. Then ask yourself what might make things a bit better. Let's say you wore your mother's favorite shoes to play in the mud. You might want to say, "I'm sorry for getting your shoes muddy. It wasn't very nice. I'll clean them off right away and I'll try to make better footwear choices in the future."

MEAN WHAT YOU SAY

This is the most important part! Don't say "sorry" to get out of trouble. And don't say it because it's what you're supposed to do. Say it because you're actually sorry. If you don't believe it, why will anyone else?

WHAT TO GIVE AN ADULT

AS A PRESENT

Your dad's birthday is just around the corner. Your grandma just graduated from the FBI academy. Your favorite teacher won the local rodeo. You want to give them presents, but what the heck do they want?

This is a tough one, I know.

I'm sorry to report that the problem never goes away. Even adults have trouble buying presents for other adults. Ever wonder why there are so many candle stores out there? Everyone loooooooves a smelly candle, right? *Wrong.* These stores exist because few people know how to buy a good present.

GOOD PRESENTS DON'T HAVE TO BE EXPENSIVE.

(In fact, many of them cost nothing at all!) **Finding a good present only takes one thing: *thought*.** That's why you'll hear people say it's the thought that counts. Usually they only say that when something goes horribly wrong. Fortunately, there's an easy way to make sure things (almost) always go right.

A PRESENT IS YOUR WAY TO SHOW SOMEONE HOW WELL YOU KNOW THEM.

The trouble starts when we ask ourselves the question, "What would they like?" That's the wrong question. **It's really hard to know what someone will like. A better question to ask is, "How can I make them happy?"** That's what you're really after, isn't it? Good, because it's not very hard to make your favorite adult happy.

STEP 1: MAKE A CARD

That's right—*make* a card. Don't buy one. Grab some paper and some markers and get to work. It doesn't matter if you're not the best artist in the world. Draw something they love. (I'd recommend a picture of you and the adult, but if that doesn't work for you, most people love koalas.) Then open it up and write something nice on the inside.

STEP 2: MAKE THEM HAPPY

Sometimes *things* can make people happy. I'm not going to lie—if you gave me some diamond earrings right now, I'd be pretty darn thrilled. But what people (especially moms and dads) really want from kids are *memories*. Find a way to show the person how much you appreciate them. Write a song in their honor. Make their favorite breakfast and carry it to them in bed (they probably want to sleep later than you do anyway). Take them to see your teacher ride in the rodeo. Those are just examples, of course. I don't know what will make your mom or dad happy. But I bet *you* do.

The memory you give them will last a lot longer than a pair of socks or a bottle of perfume.

Numba One Mom!

NEED TO DO SOMETHING NICE FOR YOUR PARENTS RIGHT AWAY?

Because you love them sooooo much.
(And because you need to get out of a little trouble?)
Here are a few quick and easy ideas!

Write them a poem. It can be a sweet, lovey-dovey poem or an adventure poem starring them as brave heroes who save the world from monsters.

Tidy up the house—always appreciated.

Give them an hour of peace by playing nicely with your little brother or sister.

Pick some flowers for a bouquet. Just don't pick the flowers out of other people's yards. You don't need to get in more trouble!

Weed the garden or rake leaves and think about how lucky you are to have a lawn. (I don't!)

Make them a sandwich. I bet they'll love one of the sandwiches in this book's special sandwich chapter (see page 34).

Make them laugh. This is my daughter's favorite trick. But you've got to wait for the right moment. If they're super mad, nothing's going to seem very funny.

WHAT TO DO iF YOU SEE SOMEONE BEiNG BULLiED

This advice will probably be more useful when you're a little bit older. But it's good to be prepared in advance!

DO YOU KNOW WHY BULLIES GET AWAY WITH WHAT THEY DO? BECAUSE OTHER PEOPLE LET THEM GET AWAY WITH IT.

While some kid is being tortured, all the other kids stand around and watch. It takes someone bold and brave to stand up for a kid who's being bullied. That's exactly what you should do.

People who watch someone else get picked on are almost as bad as the bully. **It's your job as a decent human being to make it stop.** Go get a teacher and tell them what's going on. Go get a parent. Go get your posse. Go get your big brother or sister. It doesn't matter whether the kid being picked on is your best friend or your worse enemy. If a bully is allowed to roam freely, then your school or neighborhood won't be safe for anyone.

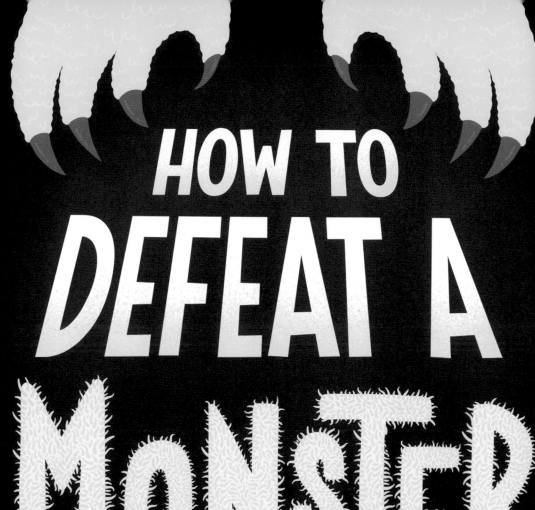

HOW TO DEFEAT A MONSTER

Oh yes, monsters exist. Real-world monsters may not have scales or 6 arms or long, pointy teeth— but that doesn't mean they're not horrible.

Real-world monsters are what keep you up all night worrying. They're the things that give you nightmares—or make you want to hide in bed all day with the covers pulled up over your head. We all meet plenty of monsters throughout our lives. They might take the form of a bully. Or a test that you're told will mean *everything*. Or a coach who wants to win just a *little* too much. Whatever your monster may be, here's how you defeat it:

1. DO SOME DETECTIVE WORK

Find out everything you can about your monster and figure out what you'll need to face it. I'm not talking about swords or anything silly like that. Information is the most powerful weapon. A monster test will be easier to beat if you know what's going to be on it. A bully may be less frightening if you discover the silly nickname her parents call her. Who knows what you'll find when you turn detective? Maybe you'll learn something that makes you laugh. Or maybe you'll get lucky and . . .

2. FIND THE MONSTER'S WEAK SPOT

Just as every dragon has a soft spot, the monsters you'll face are likely to have a weakness, too. Your cold-hearted Spanish teacher might melt if you bring him some flan. Your big sister may think twice about teasing you the day you adopt a tarantula. Your bully might stop torturing you if you buddy up with his grandma.

3. STAND TALL

Monsters win by making you feel small. No matter what, don't let them do it. Always stand tall and they'll never truly defeat you.

4. BUT DON'T BE AFRAID TO BE SCARED

People often think you can't be brave and scared at the same time. They couldn't be more wrong! In order to be brave, you HAVE to be scared! Being brave means you're smart enough to be scared—but tough enough to do what you need to do anyway.

HOW TO MAKE FRIENDS WITH AN ANIMAL

You looove animals. That's awesome! You're going to make a lot of great animal friends in your life. But I'm sorry to tell you that some animals won't love you back. Others will make terrible friends. And a lot of them will bite.

58

THE SECRET TO MAKING FRIENDS WITH AN ANIMAL IS SIMPLE:
FOOD.

It doesn't matter what kind of animal it is; a tasty treat is the way to its heart. Make sure you figure out what kind of food the animal likes. (Feeding carrots to a cat won't do you much good.) Leave the food where they'll feel comfortable eating it. Most animals won't want to eat right out of your hand. (And if they have sharp teeth, you don't want them to anyway.)

Most animals you'll meet will be other people's pets. That does NOT mean they want to make new human friends. So follow these rules when you meet someone's pet for the very first time:

ASK IF THE PET IS FRIENDLY

Never forget to do this! Some of the cutest animals are also the meanest! And just like humans, animals can be grouchy if they're sick or if they've had a bad day. Sometimes they are also scared of humans they don't know. So, don't reach out to pet any animal unless the owner says it's OK.

OK?

PUT OUT YOUR HAND
AND LET IT GIVE YOU A SNIFF

This advice works well with dogs, but it can't hurt to let other animals take a sniff, too. This is how many animals figure out if *you're* friendly or not. Trying to pet them first would be like a relative you've never met before suddenly snatching you up in a hug.

PET IT FOR 3 SECONDS—THEN STOP

If the animal has sniffed you and seems OK, give it a little pet on the back or side. Don't go for their heads or rumps. (Would you like that?) When 3 seconds have gone by, pull your hand back. If the animal comes and rubs up against you, you'll know they want more. Feel free to pet away!

DO NOT PICK AN ANIMAL UP UNTIL IT'S READY

Again, would you like to be picked up by someone (or something) much bigger? Most animals don't like that either. Wait until you're the best of friends before you try to pick up a creature.

GIVE IT A TREAT

And now here we are, right back at the start. You want to make a pet love you? The answer is food! Ask the owner if it's OK, and then whip out the treats!

Also keep in mind that there are many cute, cuddly-looking animals that don't make good friends—I'm thinking about squirrels. If you know anything about squirrels, you know that they're evil and should be avoided at all costs. (OK, maybe that's just my opinion.)

WHAT TO DO iF YOU WANT A NEW PET

We're probably not related, so I can't say yes or no to a pet. But I can predict that your parents' answer will depend a great deal on how you feel about poop.

You see, all animals produce a lot of poop. Even goldfish. (*Especially* goldfish.) **Feeding a pet isn't all that difficult—as long as you remember to do it. Grooming a pet can even be fun.** Parents usually don't mind helping out with these 2 things. But dealing with cat, dog, iguana, llama, hamster, or ferret poop is a different story altogether.

SO HOW DO YOU FEEL ABOUT POOP?

Are you cool with scooping it out of a cat box twice a day? Following a dog around until it does its business—and then picking up the present it's left behind? Cleaning out a hamster cage that's filled with little black pellets that look like chocolate sprinkles but definitely don't taste like them? Then washing your hands every single time?

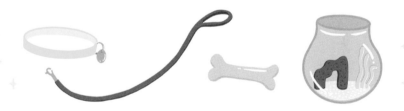

We know you've got the cuddles covered. **But if you want a pet, you'll have to prove that you're up to the nastiest, smelliest, most revolting part of the job.** Try taking care of someone else's pet for a few days and see what you think. Are you up to the poop challenge? If not, don't despair. Just try to make friends with kids who own pets. That way you get to play with the animals—and someone else gets to dispose of the poop. That's what we call a win-win situation!

YOU REALLY THINK YOU CAN HANDLE THE POOP?

Animals poop a lot more than you'd think.
Humans, for example, poop an average of 179 pounds a year!

DOGS POOP

274 pounds a year

CATS POOP

110 pounds a year

RABBITS POOP

47 pounds a year

MICE POOP

0.4 pounds a year (hey, that's not so bad!)

I can't say for sure how much GOLDFISH POOP.

But I had a goldfish for ages, and I'm pretty sure that
smelly little thing pooped AT LEAST 400 pounds a year.

WHY NOT START WITH A PET PLANT?

FIDO

Yeah, I know. Plants don't seem as exciting as animals. Until you find out that some of them eat meat! Others are masters of disguise! And a few even move when you touch them! (No joke. Read the next chapter to learn more.)

Plants are also a good way to learn how to care for a living thing—without having to clean up any poop! They need the same essentials that animal pets do:

SUNLIGHT

Plants use sunlight to make their food. (Think about that. It's amazing!) But every plant needs a different amount of sunlight. When you get your new plant pet, make sure you know whether it likes bright light or shade. If you buy your plant at a store, the information that you need is usually on a little plastic spike that's stuck in the soil.

WATER

The same thing goes for water. Plants definitely need it, but different types need different amounts. Find out how much your pet plant drinks—and don't give it any more. Watering a plant too much will kill it just as quickly as watering it too little.

FOOD

Plants use the sun to make most of their food, but they also get nourishment from the soil. This kind of food is called fertilizer, and you can add it to your plant's dirt. But make sure you know exactly what kind of fertilizer your plant likes—and exactly how much.

9 PLANTS THAT MIGHT MAKE GOOD PETS

CARNIVOROUS PLANTS

You've heard of Venus flytraps or pitcher plants? They eat meat! (If you consider bugs meat.) Don't worry—they won't bite off any of your fingers. Which is one of the many reasons they make excellent pets!

TOMATO PLANTS

Here's a fact your parents might not know: Believe it or not, tomato plants are carnivorous, too! Those little hairs on their stalks? They capture bugs and guide the dead insects down to the ground where they become the plant's fertilizer. Cool, right? And they give you yummy red fruit (yes, fruit)!

LITHOPS

These plants are masters of disguise. If you didn't know they were plants, you'd think they were stones! They don't do very much, but they come in cool colors!

SUNFLOWERS

Plant a few sunflower seeds and in a couple of months, you'll have giant flowers that are taller than you are! They'll die in the fall, of course, but not before leaving you with a bag full of delicious seeds.

AIR PLANTS

Their real name is epiphytes and they don't need dirt. Seriously! They hang out in trees and get their water and nutrients from the rain and air. Because they don't need dirt, you can put them wherever you want. You can even take them on walks! (Though I wouldn't recommend it.)

SENSITIVE PLANTS

All plants move, but most of them are much, much slower than we are. But not the *Mimosa pudica* (commonly known as the sensitive plant). When you touch its open leaves, they snap shut! Not very friendly, but definitely awesome.

ALOE VERA

Aloe looks like something out of the film *Beetlejuice* (which you should definitely watch as soon as your parents let you). It's spiky and cool and if you tear off one of its fat, juicy leaves, you'll find a slimy sap that can make burns feel better!

MUSHROOMS

Yes, smarty pants, I know mushrooms aren't plants. They're fungi, which is even more awesome! I recommend getting a mushroom growing kit if you're interested. (Which will make it so much easier.)

CACTI

Cacti are the tough guys of the plant world. Most are super prickly and don't need much love, affection, or water. You won't be able to hug it, but a cactus will look great on your window shelf. And it will probably keep looking good long after it dies, which makes it perfect for 9-year-olds.

HOW TO AVOID BEING BORING*

In my opinion, the most important thing you can be in life is INTERESTING.

Being interesting lasts much longer (and goes much deeper) than being nice to look at. And let's face it—all of your other good qualities will never shine through if people fall asleep the moment you start to speak.

9 IS THE PERFECT AGE TO BEGIN BEING INTERESTING.

(Who knows—maybe you already are!) There are countless ways you can avoid being boring. Seriously—you can make it up as you go along. There really aren't any rules. But I do have a few handy tips for those of you who are just getting started on your journey to being the most fascinating kid in the second, third, or fourth grades.

READ LOTS OF BOOKS

Why? So, you'll have things to talk about! Any kind of books will do. (It'll be much more fun if you read about things that actually interest you.) I've found that books about haunted houses, lake monsters, and King Henry VIII contain lots of information that most people like to discuss.

ASK PEOPLE ABOUT THEMSELVES

You know what's really boring? People who talk about them-selves all the time. Whether you're meeting someone new or hanging out with someone you've known your whole life, the best way to keep the other person entertained is to spend at least half the time talking about them. (Don't spend all your time talking about them or they may start to wonder if you're an undercover spy.)

TRY NEW THINGS

You know what else is boring? People who do the same stuff over and over and over again. Try mixing things up. Eat foods you've never tried before. Talk to people at school you've never spoken to before. Check out new aisles in the supermarket. Wear a cape. You get the idea.

ENJOY BEING DiFFERENT

Can you imagine how dull life would be if we all looked the same way, lived in the same kinds of houses, and had the same kinds of sisters and brothers? Thankfully we don't. We're all wonderfully different—and interesting people are proud of it. Never try to be anyone but yourself.

I NEED INTERESTING FACTS!
WHAT SHOULD I READ ABOUT?

I've got you covered!

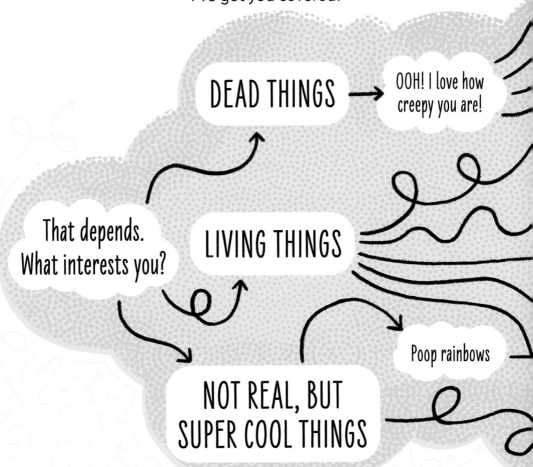

DEAD THINGS → OOH! I love how creepy you are!

That depends. What interests you?

LIVING THINGS

Poop rainbows

NOT REAL, BUT SUPER COOL THINGS

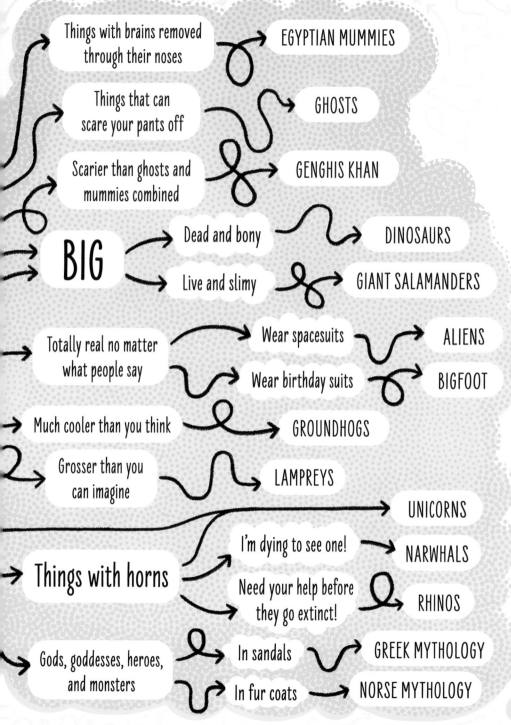

Things with brains removed through their noses → EGYPTIAN MUMMIES

Things that can scare your pants off → GHOSTS

Scarier than ghosts and mummies combined → GENGHIS KHAN

BIG
- Dead and bony → DINOSAURS
- Live and slimy → GIANT SALAMANDERS

Totally real no matter what people say
- Wear spacesuits → ALIENS
- Wear birthday suits → BIGFOOT

Much cooler than you think → GROUNDHOGS

Grosser than you can imagine → LAMPREYS

→ UNICORNS

Things with horns
- I'm dying to see one! → NARWHALS
- Need your help before they go extinct! → RHINOS

Gods, goddesses, heroes, and monsters
- In sandals → GREEK MYTHOLOGY
- In fur coats → NORSE MYTHOLOGY

HOW TO
CATCH
A
SPiDER

Before I can offer any advice, I must ask you one simple question: Are you in Australia? If your answer is yes, and you see a spider, I would suggest that you run.

DON'T TRY TO STOMP IT.

DON'T KEEP IT AS A PET.

DON'T FEED IT FLIES HOPING IT WILL BECOME YOUR LOYAL COMPANION.

In Australia (and a few other parts of the world), creepy crawlies of any sort are not to be trifled with. (That's Australian for "They're really dangerous.")

However, if you come across a spider in the United States or many other parts of the world, the situation probably isn't quite so serious. **Yes, there are a few venomous spiders out there.** (It's a good idea to know what they look like.) There are also some huge, hairy beasts. (You won't be able to miss them.) **But most of the spiders you see in your house are just hanging around hurting no one.** Still, you probably don't want them sharing your room.

If you see a spider crawling up a wall or scurrying across the floor, you can run away screaming if you like. I've certainly shrieked at a spider or 2. **However, there are 2 good reasons for learning to capture spiders.**

FIRST**, everyone will think you're brave.**

AND SECOND**, if you can calmly deal with a spider, there's not much else you can't do.**

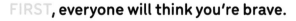

WAIT—*CATCH* THEM?
WHY NOT SQUISH THEM, YOU ASK?

I know some people think spiders are disgusting and scary, but if you go around squishing everything you don't like, you won't have much time for anything else, and your shoes will probably be ruined. Plus, spiders help us by eating bugs we like even less (like mosquitoes). So . . .

GRAB A GLASS OR CLEAR CONTAINER

Put the container on top of the spider. (The clear part is important. You want to make sure you've actually captured the spider, and it hasn't crawled into your shoe.) The spider will go a bit nuts when it realizes it's been trapped. Don't freak out! Catch your breath and have a good look. This is your chance to see a spider up close!

NOW FIND A STIFF SHEET OF PAPER

A piece of notebook paper won't do. Try to use a flimsy piece of paper, and you're likely to set your spider free. No, you need a thin but sturdy piece—like the cover of a magazine or the jacket of a book. (Just not *this* book.) Slowly slide the piece of paper under the rim of your container. Once the paper is all the way under the rim, wait for the spider to crawl up to the top of the container. Then slide your fingers under the paper and FLIP! Turn the container over with the paper still over the top.

RELEASE YOUR SPIDER INTO THE WILD

If you're super cool, you'll take the spider outside and gently release it onto a piece of grass. If you're like me, you'll set your container down, knock the paper off with the tip of your shoe and quickly get out of the way. (Running and screaming as much as you like!)

WHAT TO DO iF YOU'RE STUNG BY A HONEYBEE

There are lots of different kinds of bees, of course. Some, like hornets and wasps, are worse than others. If you spot a hornet or a wasp nest, you'll want to hit the road fast.

Honeybees (you know the ones—yellow and black and fuzzy) are going to be pretty hard to avoid. They're everywhere! And that's exactly where we want them to be. **Honeybees pollinate many of the plants we eat.** Without them, we wouldn't have fruits or vegetables!

BUT LIKE MOST GOOD THINGS, HONEYBEES COME WITH A DOWNSIDE.

IF YOU MESS WITH THEM, THEY'LL STING YOU.

So the best thing to do is leave them alone. If you see one, don't swat at it or scream at the top of your lungs. Honeybees fly slowly, so it's easy to make an escape. Just calmly walk away (or run if you have to) and let it go about its business.

Most of the time, stings happen by accident. (That's why it's good to wear shoes when you see bees around.) But no matter how careful you are, at some point in your life, you're probably gonna get stung. Here's what you do when that happens:

KEEP YOUR COOL!

Yes, it will hurt, but probably not as much as you think. And probably not for as long as you imagine.

GET THE STINGER OUT

When a honeybee stings, it loses its stinger. (It also loses its guts in the process—which is why honeybees die as soon as they sting. If it makes you feel any better, they have it *way* worse than you.) You need to get the stinger out ASAP. Use the edge of a butter knife to scrape the stinger out of your skin. Don't use your fingernails or tweezers! If you squeeze the stinger, it could send more venom into your skin.

WASH THE STING AND TRY A HOME REMEDY

Make sure you wash the bee sting well with soap and water. Then raid your cupboards for remedies. Some people claim toothpaste will make a bee sting feel better. Others will tell you to try apple cider vinegar, baking soda, or honey. To be honest, you'll probably end up using calamine lotion (the pink stuff), but why not make an experiment out of it?

PUT SOMETHING COLD ON THE STING

A bag of frozen peas would be perfect, but anything cold will do. Just be careful putting anything icy right against your skin. You don't want a bee sting AND frostbite.

HAVE SOME ICE CREAM

Your parents will feel sorry for you, so this is an excellent time to ask for some.

LET SOMEONE KNOW IF YOU START FEELING TERRIBLE

Most people are not allergic to honeybee stings. But there are a few people who might need to see a doctor right away. If you start feeling sick or dizzy or have trouble breathing, let an adult know immediately.

BE PROUD OF YOURSELF

Bee stings are part of growing up. Most of us never get stung more than once or twice. Hopefully you've gotten your stings out of the way!

HOW TO KEEP YOUR HEAD BUG-FREE

It's not the end of the world if you get lice.
The odds are pretty good that you will one day.
But like many other things in life (such as snakes
and marshmallow fluff), lice are best avoided.

SHARING ISN'T ALWAYS CARING

Yes, I know you've been told it's nice to share. Most of the time, that's true. But not when it comes to lice. The easiest way to end up with a head full of bugs is to borrow or lend hats, hoods, brushes, or hair accessories. So, even if your BFF is begging to borrow your cute new headband, the most caring thing you can do is say no.

BUGS LOVE HATS

Would you stick your head in an anthill? Use a spider's web as a hood? Of course not. Then why would you put on a hat that's not yours when there's a very good chance that it's brimming with bugs?! Want to avoid lice? Then don't try on hats. Period. It doesn't matter if they're in a dress-up box or a store.

BUGS LOVE HELMETS, TOO

There may come a time when you need to borrow a helmet. Protecting your brain is more important than avoiding lice, so here's what to do: Buy a plastic shower cap and put it over your hair before you put on the helmet. It's not perfect, but it's definitely better than nothing.

WHAT TO DO IF YOU START TO ITCH

Don't keep it to yourself! Tell a parent right away! Lice aren't going to go away on their own. The longer you wait, the more bugs you'll have.

CAN I TOUCH...

A dead bird outside?

Only with rubber gloves on and only for scientific purposes.

A dead bird in the kitchen?

No problem. But wash your hands well before and afterwards.

A dog I've just met?

After you've asked the owner if he's friendly.

That pot on the stove?

If you like the skin on your hands, make sure it's not flaming hot first.

Someone else's privates?

Nope! And if someone asks you to touch theirs, tell your parents right away.

My privates?

Sure. They belong to you, don't they? But there's a reason they're called privates. If you touch them, try to do it when you're alone.

A subway pole?

There are few things grosser than a subway pole, but sometimes you have to grab hold. These are the situations that hand sanitizer was made for.

A public toilet seat?

Oh geez. Only if it's absolutely necessary. If it is, wipe off the seat and cover it in lots of toilet paper. This isn't the time to save trees.

DO YOU HAVE WHAT iT TO TAKES BE

THE
MOST
iNTERESTiNG
KiD
iN TOWN

(OR AT LEAST YOUR HOUSE)?

CHECK ALL THAT APPLY:

- ☐ I HAVE AT LEAST ONE UNUSUAL AND SURPRISING SKILL.
- ☐ I HAVE SEEN A GHOST.
- ☐ I KNOW WHAT'S IN SNOT AND I MAKE A MEAN FAKE BOOGER.
- ☐ I KNOW AT LEAST ONE AMAZING JOKE.
- ☐ I MAKE FRIENDS WITH KIDS WHO AREN'T JUST LIKE ME.
- ☐ I CAN WHIP UP THE WORLD'S BEST SANDWICH.
- ☐ I HAVE AN AWESOME PET PLANT.
- ☐ I'M NOT AFRAID TO CATCH SPIDERS OUTSIDE OF AUSTRALIA.
- ☐ I HAVE SOLVED AT LEAST ONE CRIME.
- ☐ I CAN GET GUM OUT OF MY HAIR BEFORE MY PARENTS FIND OUT.
- ☐ I KNOW ALL THE BEST HIDING SPOTS.
- ☐ I MAY BE IN DISGUISE.
- ☐ I ALWAYS KEEP AN EYE OUT FOR HIDDEN TREASURE.
- ☐ I KNOW WHAT A MERMAID'S PURSE IS.
- ☐ I READ INTERESTING BOOKS.
- ☐ I CAN MAKE FRIENDS WITH AN ANIMAL.
- ☐ I'M AN ACE WITH A VACUUM CLEANER.
- ☐ I KNOW HOW TO DEFEAT MONSTERS AND BULLIES.
- ☐ I KNOW WHAT TO DO IF SOMEONE'S BLEEDING OR CHOKING.
- ☐ I LIKE BEING DIFFERENT.
- ☐ I WOULDN'T WANT TO BE ANYONE OTHER THAN ME.

It doesn't matter how many you checked.
I promise you have what it takes!

NEED
A COOL AND SURPRISING
NEW SKILL?

GIRL

GREAT! Are you a girl or a boy? → *Whatever. Moving on!*

How will you use your new skill?

BOY

IMPRESS OTHER 9-YEAR-OLDS

Fast, easy → Old-fashioned → WHISTLE WITH FINGERS

High-tech → GIF MAKING

Hard, worth it → Creepy → HALLOWEEN MAKEUP

Edgy → LOCK PICKING

LOOK FANCY → How do you feel about perfume and croissants?

I'd rather walk the plank → SAILING

❤ → SPEAK FRENCH

SAVE LIVES

Other peoples' → CPR

My own → At home → FIXING TOILETS

From bad guys → SELF-DEFENSE

FIGHT CRIME → Cape or no cape?

No cape → Superpowers?

NO → SELF-DEFENSE

YES → ONE-LINERS

Def cape! → SEWING

TAKE OVER THE WORLD → Use your powers for good, not evil! → CODING

93

HOW TO TELL iF SOMEONE iS

BAD NEWS

You've probably heard someone described as
"BAD NEWS."
**(I really hope it wasn't you!) If a person is
"bad news," you should do your best to avoid them.**

The problem is, you can't tell if someone's bad news just by looking at them. Some of the nicest people I know have scary tattoos, nose rings, and look like they might wrestle bears for a living. **If you judge people on their appearance, you could end up missing out on some of the best friends you've ever had.**

If you want to know who's really "bad news," you're going to have to watch the way people *act*. Lucky for all us, there are a few simple ways to quickly figure out if someone should be avoided.

THEY'RE MEAN TO PEOPLE WHO ARE YOUNGER OR DIFFERENT

Do they pick on little kids? Do they make fun of people for things they can't change (like braces, belt size, or big hairy moles)? This is a sure sign that someone's a bully—even if they're nice to *you*. If you think you can convince them to cut it out, go ahead and try! (Sometimes people just need to be told what they're doing is wrong.) But if they won't listen, stay away! (And follow the rules on page 54 about what to do when you see someone bullied!)

THEY'RE MEAN TO ANIMALS

Why would anyone be cruel to a harmless animal? It boggles my mind! If you see someone taunting a dog, kicking a cat, or mistreating any other animal, you *definitely* don't want to be friends with them.

THEY LITTER

Do you know someone who drops their trash on the ground or doesn't pick up after their dog? I'd think twice about making friends with them. Littering doesn't make someone *mean*. But it does tell you that a person may be lazy and selfish. Become friends with a litterer, and you'll probably spend a lot of time cleaning up after their messes.

HOW TO MAKE PEOPLE THINK YOU'RE GOOD NEWS

Sometimes life isn't as complicated as it seems. If you're nice to people, they'll probably be nice to you, too. (People who aren't nice in return are BAD NEWS.) If you want to be known as GOOD NEWS, here's what to do:

BE NICE TO YOUR RELATIVES.

ALWAYS STAND UP FOR THE LITTLE GUY.

OPEN DOORS FOR OTHER PEOPLE.

DON'T MAKE PEOPLE CLEAN UP YOUR MESSES.

IF YOU'RE HAVING FUN, INVITE EVERYONE TO JOIN.

DON'T MAKE OTHER PEOPLE FEEL LEFT OUT.

BE FRIENDS WITH THE SHY KID, THE NEW KID,
AND THE KID WHO ISN'T LIKE EVERYONE ELSE.

MAKE FRIENDS WITH THE PEOPLE WHO WORK AT YOUR
SCHOOL.

ALWAYS SAY THANK YOU.

BE INTERESTED IN OTHER PEOPLE.

IF YOU SEE A KID WHO NEEDS HELP, GIVE IT TO THEM.

HOW TO SOLVE A CRIME

You probably won't have the opportunity to investigate any gory, gruesome stuff. (The police are really picky about who's allowed to help.) But there's still work to do! Countless crimes are commited in the average home every year—and many of them go unsolved.

Let's say your mother discovers a nasty stain on the brand-new carpet. (A crime, by the way, that is easily concealed once you know how.) Someone's going to be blamed and possibly punished for the mess! And unless you solve the crime, it could end up being you!

STUDY THE CRIME SCENE

Act quickly and don't touch anything! Take pictures before anyone has a chance to mess with the evidence! How big is the stain? Is there a bowl or a glass nearby? Is there an embarrassed-looking pet in the room? How about a grinning toddler? (Grinning toddlers are responsible for most stain-related crimes.)

GATHER EViDENCE

Put on a pair of rubber gloves. (There are probably some under your sink. No, winter gloves won't cut it.) If you've found any clues (a container, a diaper, a written confession), place your evidence in a plastic bag. You may want to dust for fingerprints later.

Once you've finished, get down on your hands and knees. You're not going to like this part, I'm afraid. You're going to have to smell the stain. There's a chance it's something like apple juice that smells pretty good. But odds are, it's going to reek. If your nose can't identify the liquid, use a cotton swab to take a sample. Place the sample in a plastic bag.

INTERVIEW WITNESSES

Next, talk to all the people who were in the house when the crime took place. Record their statements. Does anyone seem suspicious? Can everyone keep their stories straight?

DOCUMENT YOUR FINDINGS

Write down what you've discovered and attach photos as proof. For instance:

At 8:25 am on Tuesday the 18th, Mom (age 40) found a giant stain on the new carpet. A dry diaper was discovered stuffed beneath the couch cushion, and a grinning toddler was spotted nearby. When I sniffed the stain, my nose was able to identify the liquid as PEE. Charlie (age 2) refused to confess but he continued to grin suspiciously. Dad (age 40) admitted that he had lost track of Charlie for approximately 3 minutes around 8:19 am.

MAKE YOUR CASE

You have photos. You have evidence. You have witness testimony. Now you can draw your conclusions. Charlie took off his diaper and peed on the floor. Crime solved. Your family can finally move on.

HOW TO BE A DETECTIVE WHEREVER YOU GO

The best detectives see things that other people overlook. A fun, easy way to train yourself to notice these little details is to have a scavenger hunt every day. No matter where you are, there's always something cool you can look for!

Hi8HWAY

- License plates from every state

- People who look like they might be on the run from the law

CiTY

- Green Men (cool carvings of men with faces made out of leaves—they can be found on buildings and churches)

- Rats

- Mushrooms (look, don't touch)

- People who may be extraterrestrials in disguise

- Evil squirrels (or good ones—*yawn*)

- Street art

COUNTRYSIDE

- Mushrooms (remember, don't touch)

  - Gnomes and fairies

- Poisonous plants (look, don't touch)

  - Weird bugs

- Pretty birds (or ugly ones—your call)

  - Fossils

BEACH

- Shells

- Sea glass

- Mermaid's purses (shark egg cases)

- Sea monster scales

- Shark teeth

WHAT TO DO iF YOU'RE BLEEDING

When I was growing up, I knew a couple of kids who would faint at the sight of blood. I always felt sorry for them. We've all got red stuff sloshing around in our veins, and it doesn't matter how careful you are—some of that blood is eventually going to leak out.

JUST A SMiDGE

You probably scraped your knee or stapled your thumb. I'm sure it hurts like heck, but you're definitely going to survive. Make sure you wash it first. Put some hydrogen peroxide on the wound, add a little Neosporin, and top it off with a Band-Aid. That's it! You're done! Start applying to medical schools!

MORE THAN A SMIDGE— LESS THAN A GUSHER

OK, it's getting a bit more serious, but you can handle this, too. Wash the wound as soon as you can. Then apply a bandage and put pressure on it. It may take a little while for the blood to stop, but as long as it's not gushing out, you're on the right track. When the bleeding slows down, follow the instructions above.

OM8, iT'S ALL OVER THE PLACE

If you're bleeding like crazy, it's time to get help fast. It going to be scary, but you've got to stay calm. Make a bandage out of whatever fabric you can find. Rip your shirt if you have to. Place pressure on the wound and, if possible, keep it raised above your head. Call 911—or have someone else call for you. Tell them how you hurt yourself and where they can find you.

WHEN iT'S SOMEONE ELSE'S BLOOD . . .

If you see someone who's seriously hurt, it's your job to help. If you have a phone, call 911. Don't wait for someone else to do it. Again, the secret is staying calm. Tell the person on the other end of the line what's happened and exactly where you are. Give them as much information as you can. If you don't have a phone, find a trusted adult who does.

HOW TO SAVE SOMEONE WHO'S CHOKING

(INCLUDING YOURSELF!)

If you end up saving someone's life before you turn 18, odds are this is the way you'll do it. Choking kills thousands of people every year. But there's a simple move you can learn that could mean the difference between life and death. You've probably heard of it. **It's called the Heimlich maneuver.**

Your arms may not be long enough to perform the maneuver on adults, but they're the perfect length to save people your age or younger. Read the instructions on the next page and practice getting into position. But DON'T perform the Heimlich on people who aren't choking. And never give a baby the Heimlich—they're too small and breakable.

UNIVERSAL SIGN FOR CHOKING

How do you know if someone is choking? They'll be gasping for air, with their hands around their throats, unable to speak. If that's what's happening, here's what to do.

1. MAKE THE PERSON STAND UP.

2. BEND THEM FORWARD A BIT AND USE THE HEEL OF YOUR HAND TO GIVE THEM 5 HARD WHACKS ON THE BACK. THIS MIGHT BE ENOUGH TO KNOCK THE FOOD OUT.

3. IF NOT, GET BEHIND THE PERSON AND WRAP YOUR ARMS AROUND THEIR WAIST.

4. MAKE A FIST WITH ONE HAND. PUT IT RIGHT ABOVE THEIR BELLY BUTTON WITH YOUR THUMB STICKING INTO THEIR STOMACH.

5. GRAB THE FIST WITH YOUR OTHER HAND.

6. WITH A QUICK, POWERFUL MOVEMENT, PULL YOUR FISTS BACKWARD AND UPWARD, INTO THEIR STOMACH.

7. MAKE THE SAME MOVEMENT 5 TIMES IN A ROW.

8. KEEP DOING IT UNTIL THE PERSON CAN BREATHE.

If you're the one choking and there's no one around, perform the same movement on yourself 5 times in a row. Keep doing it until the food in your throat comes free. If that doesn't work, try ramming the upper part of your belly (just beneath the ribs) into the arm of a chair, the side of a table, or some other hard surface.

1.

2.

3.

4.

5.

6.

7.

8.

WHAT TO DO iF THERE iS GUM iN YOUR HAiR

You blow a bubble as big as your head. Then *POP!* It's all over your face. Not only that, it's in your hair, your eyelashes, and your mustache. (You probably don't have to worry about mustaches yet, but who knows!) It's a total disaster.

You can either shave your whole head—or you can tell an adult. Neither seems like a good solution. You love your hair and you'd rather keep it—but you hate getting lectures from adults even more. (And let's be honest, this probably isn't the first time you've gotten gum stuck in your hair.)

Thankfully, there's a third solution! Now that you're 9, you're old enough to get the gum out ALL BY YOURSELF. (Or perhaps with the help of a trusted friend.) It's actually pretty easy, but it can get terribly messy. So be prepared to take a nice, long shower afterwards!

GET SOMETHING GREASY

Peanut butter is the classic choice, but vegetable oil or olive oil work well, too. In a pinch, a nice vinaigrette salad dressing should do the trick.

DON'T RUIN YOUR CLOTHES

Ever seen what peanut butter can do to a shirt? Yeah, it's not pretty. So, unless you want to explain a ruined shirt to your parents (possibly even worse than gum in your hair), take it off—or cover it up with a garbage bag.

SPREAD THE GOOP AROUND

Separate the gummed-up hair from the rest. Then rub the peanut butter or oil into the hair that's above and below the gum. (This will keep the gum from spreading.) When you're done, start rubbing the peanut butter into the gum itself.

WAIT PATIENTLY

Sitting in the bathroom with no shirt on and hair covered in peanut butter is not going to be fun. But you gotta give the stuff a few minutes to work! (Usually 5 will do.)

COMB IT OUT AND WASH

Use a comb (not a brush, for heaven's sake!) to pull the gum out of your hair. If you don't have a comb, just use your fingers! When the gum is gone, jump in the shower and give your hair a wash. Make sure you do a really good job; if you don't want your parents to be suspicious, it's probably not a good idea to smell like a sandwich.

HOW TO PLAN YOUR ESCAPE

You lead a life of adventure. I can only imagine what kind of thrilling situations you'll find yourself in this year!

Maybe you'll be on the run from ninjas. Or chasing tornados across the Great Plains. Or perhaps you'll find yourself in a situation that's a little more common—like facing a fire or a furious sibling. It doesn't matter what kind of trouble you find yourself in.

WHEN iT C⊖MES TO GETTiNG ⊖UT ALIVE, ONE THING iS WAY MORE iMPORTANT THAN EVERYTHING ELSE:
IF YOU WANT T⊖ SURVIVE, YOU'RE G⊖iNG TO NEED A PLAN.

So how do you come up with a plan if you don't know what's going to happen—or when? Excellent question!

The fact is, most of the best plans require 1 of 2 things:

ESCAPING (fire) or HIDING (furious sibling).

You spend almost all of your time in a just a couple of places. Home, school, and the International Spy Museum in Washington, D.C. (No? Maybe that's just me. Come up with your own list!) Take a little time and figure out your escape routes in each of these places.

DO YOU KNOW WHERE ALL THE EXITS ARE?

CAN YOU CLIMB OUT OF THE WINDOWS?

Come up with a few different options if you can.

ONCE YOU HAVE YOUR ESCAPE ROUTE MEMORIZED, START LOOKING FOR GOOD HIDING SPOTS.

This is one of your biggest advantages as a 9-year-old—you can cram yourself into places no adult will ever fit into! (This is also excellent training for advanced hide-and-go-seek.)

As soon as you get the hang of it, looking for escape routes and hiding spots can be fun. **Wherever you go, pretend you're the star of an action movie.** And after you've done your research, be sure to relax. The wonderful thing about having a plan is that once you know what it is, you don't need to worry. You've already thought ahead!

HOW TO MAKE FAKE POOP

You're 9, so pranks are probably a big part of your life by now, and fake poop is a classic prank. You can buy plastic poop, of course, but where's the fun in that? Why not make your own?

I happen to think fake poop is funniest when it's made out of something you're able to eat. Can you imagine your parents' faces if you picked up something that looked like poop and took a big bite out of it? That's quality entertainment right there, my friends.

MAKING EDIBLE POOP IS INCREDIBLY EASY.

Any brown food can be molded into something that looks like it was left behind by a dog (or bear, baby, cat, or raccoon). However, there are few things as convincing—or delicious—as poop made out of a Snickers bar.

You'll need to melt it a bit in order to mold it into the right shape. This doesn't require a stove. Just put the Snickers on a plate and leave it in the sun for a few minutes. Or place the plate near a heater in the wintertime.

Once it's soft, mix it up a bit (you'll want some of the peanuts showing) and then sculpt your masterpiece.

When you're done, cut out a piece of waxed paper
that matches the shape of your poop perfectly. (This
way you won't have to put it directly on the floor.)

Wait for the perfect moment—when someone is passing
by—then pick it up and take a bite! (As with all pranks,
this only works on adults with senses of humor.)

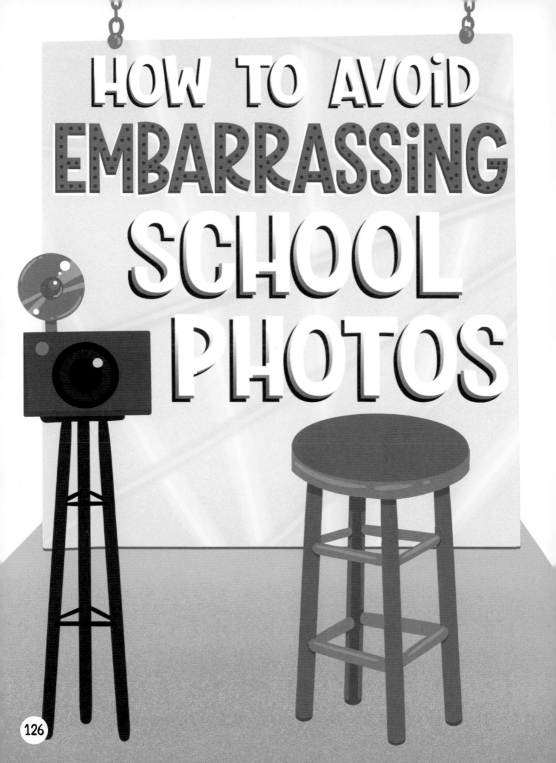

IT CAN HAPPEN TO ANYONE

School picture day comes and goes. You think everything's fine. Then a few weeks later, an envelope arrives in the mail. Inside are pictures of someone who's wearing the very same clothes you wore on picture day. They have the same shade of hair and freckles in all the same places. But it *can't* be you, because the kid in the photos is downright *hideous*.

At one point or another, everyone's hideous picture twin will try to slip into their school photos. Mine got the better of me in the fourth and fifth grades—until I finally learned how to outwit her.

BE READY

Soon after school starts in the fall, the school photo announcement will be made. *Mark the date on your calendar!* Your hideous picture twin is always waiting to catch you off guard. If you don't remember when photo day is, you can bet your butt he or she WILL. Be sure to plan what you're going to wear on the big day—and make sure it's not the same thing you wore last year!

BE CLEAN

You know what? Why not follow this suggestion every day of the year? Take a bath if you need one. Make sure your hair is combed. Brush your teeth in the morning. (And make sure there's nothing stuck between them when you pose!) Your hideous twin loves nothing more than greasy hair and a peanut butter–coated tooth.

BE COMFORTABLE

You're not going to have your picture taken the second you walk into school. And whatever you choose to wear, you'll have to wear it all day. It doesn't matter how good that stiff dress or those tight shoes look in the morning. By the time your picture gets snapped, you'll be so distracted that your hideous twin will have no trouble at all slipping into the portrait.

BE HAPPY

Forget saying cheese when you get in front of the camera. Nothing will bring out your hideous twin like a fake smile. So, before you leave for school in the morning, think of the funniest joke you've ever been told. Then, as you pose for photographer, repeat the punch line in your head. Your smile will be real, your eyes will sparkle, your face will glow—and your hideous twin will be banished for good.

BE YOU

Just *relax*. Don't break into your big sister's makeup or try on every outfit in your closet. Your school photo is supposed to be a picture of YOU. So just be yourself! And if your hideous twin manages to steal your spot, don't despair. Everyone has a photo (or 2) of their hideous twin—and someday it will be the one that makes you smile the most.

HOW TO GO UNDERCOVER

I'm not going to ask you why you want to disguise your appearance. You have very good reasons, I'm sure. I just hope that, when you've finished reading this chapter, you'll use your skills for the good of all humankind.

When it comes to disguising their appearance, most people make the same mistakes. They just put on a wig and a crazy outfit. Perhaps if they're feeling creative, they'll add a fake mole or crooked teeth. This is NOT the right way to go undercover. You'll be spotted in a second!

TRY NOT TO LOOK LIKE YOURSELF

Did you just say "Duh"? I bet you did. But I promise you it's excellent advice. There are certain things about each of us that make us easy to recognize. Maybe it's your hair, your nose, or even the way you walk. (Ask a friend if you're not sure.) These are the things you'll need to change.

LITTLE CHANGES GO A LONG WAY

Let's say you need to change your hair, your nose, and the way you walk.

1. Put on a hat to hide your hair. (Make sure it's right for the season and isn't filled with lice—see page 86.) Or wear your hair in a different style.

2. You can't do much about your nose, but a pair of glasses (with clear lenses) will change the whole look of your face. Stuff a cotton ball or 2 into your cheeks if you really want to see a big difference.

3. Slip a pebble in your shoe and it will totally change the way you walk.

LOOK AS BORING AS POSSIBLE

The best way to go unrecognized is to make sure no one looks at you at all! Don't wear anything that will call attention to you. That means no clothing with writing on it, no bright colors, no weird styles, and no trench coats. Also, be sure to leave your favorite clothes at home. (People will recognize them right away!)

There are lots of good reasons to leave your bed messy each morning. Maybe no one else cares (lucky you). Maybe you figure you'll just get back into it later. I totally understand! When I was 9, I would have said the very same things.

IT'S AN EASY WAY TO START GETTING STUFF DONE

You have a ton of things to do every day, am I right? And let's face it, a lot of them are probably hard (math homework) or annoying (math homework). You've got to get started, but you aren't ready to tackle the big stuff right away. So, start with something small! Making your bed is one of the easiest things you'll do all day. It only takes a couple of minutes, but it makes you feel like you've accomplished something right after you roll out of bed!

IT PROTECTS YOU FROM PRANKS, PETS, AND PESTS

Not convinced by that last one? OK, here's another reason. If your bed's made, you'll be able to see if something's inside it. There is nothing worse than climbing into a bed with rumpled covers and feeling your feet brush up against something warm and furry. (Cold and wet is equally horrifying.)

MAKING YOUR BED?

But now I know how horribly wrong I was. There are at least 4 excellent reasons to tuck in your sheets and pull up your covers each morning.

IT COULD MAKE YOUR PARENTS HAPPY

Making your bed makes it look like you've cleaned your room. (Without actually cleaning your room!) As we all know, clean rooms make parents happy. And happy parents are MUCH more fun to be around. Get your mom and dad in a good mood first thing in the morning, and there's a much better chance that your day will be great.

A WELL-MADE BED FEELS SOOOOO GOOD

I can't think of a better way to end the day than snuggling up under clean sheets and tidy blankets. It's like giving yourself a present for making it through another day. Not only that, but people sleep better in a well-made bed—and getting a good night's sleep is the very best way to make sure tomorrow is awesome.

WHERE TO LOOK FOR

HiDDEN TREASURE

You don't need a pirate's map to search for hidden treasure. There's valuable stuff around us that never gets found—because nobody bothers to look!

THERE ARE 2 TYPES OF PEOPLE WHO FIND HIDDEN TREASURE:
PEOPLE WHO GET LUCKY, AND CURIOUS PEOPLE.

You can't *choose* to be lucky. You either are or (like most of us) you're not. But you *can* decide to be the sort of curious person who investigates every nook and cranny and searches every forgotten place.

Back in the olden days, people often buried their treasures—and forgot to come back for them. If you can get your hands on a metal detector, make sure you search your backyard! (If you don't have a metal detector lying around your house, you can make one using a radio and a calculator. The instructions are easy to find online. (Ask a parent to get them for you.) Here are a few other places you might want to look:

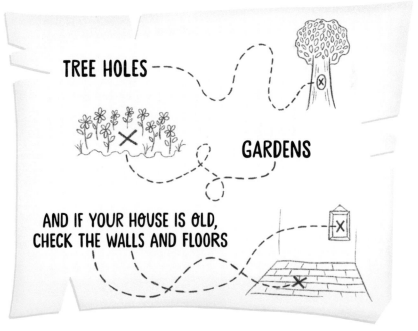

TREE HOLES

GARDENS

AND IF YOUR HOUSE IS OLD, CHECK THE WALLS AND FLOORS

Sometimes people don't even know they have treasure. They'll forget they have it—or even give it away! Treasure hunters have found priceless paintings and other valuables at or in these places:

ATTICS

THRIFT STORES

BARNS

GARAGE SALES

FLEA MARKETS

Even if you don't find diamonds, rubies, and doubloons, you can probably fill your piggy bank if you regularly check:

COUCH CUSHIONS

WASHING MACHINES

YOUR HAMPER

JUNK DRAWERS

YOUR OLD BACKPACKS

YOUR COAT POCKETS

PARKING METERS

VENDING MACHINES

A FEW THINGS YOU SHOULD KNOW HOW TO USE

You're 9. It's a great age to become a responsible human being. Oh, I'm sorry, does that sound boring? It shouldn't, because being a responsible human being means you get to use some pretty awesome gadgets.

FIRE EXTINGUISHERS

I've never had to use a fire extinguisher, thank goodness. (I'm itching to try one out.) Find the one in your house. If you don't have one, ask your parents to buy one. Then read the instructions and be prepared! (Don't test it if there isn't a fire, unless you want to get into very big trouble.)

DISHWASHERS

The secret to an amazing dishwasher experience is SCRAPING YOUR PLATE. The machine's supposed to wash dishes—not eat your leftovers. Make sure there's enough room between the dishes for water to reach them. Now fill the drawer labeled DETERGENT with . . . wait for it . . . *detergent*. Maybe your dishwasher will ask you what sort of cycle you want. If it does, a safe choice is "normal." Then hit start! Maybe it will not ask what sort of cycle you want. Then hit start!

VACUUM CLEANERS

Being handy with a vacuum cleaner will get you out of ALL SORTS OF TROUBLE. They're very good at sucking up the remains of the dishes you broke or the sprinkles you spilled while sneaking a bowl of ice cream. Just don't suck up anything big, wet, or alive and you should be fine. And make sure you know how to change the bag—just in case one day you make a REALLY big mess.

MiCROWAVES

You're probably not allowed to use the microwave yet. But just in case you are, the most important thing to know is that there are many things you should NEVER EVER EVER put inside them. Do not put anything metal (including silverware, cans, or aluminum foil) into a microwave. Do not put anything living (including hamsters or toads) in there either. Eggs will explode, as will grapes, bananas, and uncovered liquids. Sure, that sounds entertaining—until you have to clean it up. And believe me, your parents aren't going to do it for you.

ROBOTS

You don't have robot yet? What are you waiting for?
Go make one!

THE BIGGEST SECRET IN ★ THE WORLD

I CAN'T BELIEVE THAT EVERYONE ON EARTH HASN'T FIGURED THIS ONE OUT YET.

I'm sad to say that when I was 9 years old, I hadn't figured it out, either. **Looking back, I can only imagine how much easier my life could have been if someone had told me THE SECRET.**

HERE'S THE FIRST HALF OF THE SECRET:

You're 9. That means you're cute. All 9-year-olds are cute to adults. (You're made that way so we'll tolerate you when you're super annoying.)

HERE'S THE SECOND HALF OF THE SECRET:

If you're cute AND nice, most adults will bend over backward for you. No joke. I'm talking free lollipops, baked goods—you name it.

I'm sure you don't believe me. I wouldn't have believed it, either. So, go ahead and put the secret to the test. Spend one day going out of your way to be nice to the people you meet. Smile. Say hello. Compliment their outfits. Whatever it takes. But here's the thing—it has to be real. If it seems like you're faking it, people will just think you're creepy. And creepy kids don't get free lollipops.

HOW TO FiND THE ANSWERS TO ALL TO ALL YOUR QUESTIONS

You will never know everything. No matter how old you get, you're still going to have lots of questions. Which is awesome! That means that even when you're 109, there will still be things left to discover.

What's NOT awesome is that a lot of us never ask the questions that pop into our heads. There might be something we really, really, really want to know, but we're too shy to ask. We start worrying that asking will make us look dumb. Or that other people will think our question is silly.

The truth is, asking questions doesn't make you look dumb. It makes you look INTERESTED. And every time you ask a question, you get a little bit smarter. In fact, the smartest people in the world are the people who ask the MOST questions! That's how they got that way!

The trick is finding the right person to ask. If you want to know why your pee is bright green, a good person to ask is a doctor. If you want to know if goats make good friends, a good person to ask is a farmer. But there is ONE person you can ask almost anything. They might not know the answer—but they'll know where to find it! That person is . . . A LIBRARIAN. That's why libraries exist—to answer all your questions.

So, the next time you have a question burning deep inside of you, head straight to your library and ASK!

TEN THINGS
YOU SHOULD DO BEFORE YOU
TURN

10
(IF YOU HAVEN'T ALREADY)

1. PACK YOUR OWN SUITCASE THE NEXT TIME YOU GO ON A TRIP.

2. TRAIN YOURSELF TO WALK THROUGH YOUR
HOUSE WITHOUT MAKING A SOUND.

3. LEARN HOW TO READ A MAP.

4. KEEP A PLANT ALIVE.

5. EARN MONEY FOR DOING AN ODD JOB.
(NO, CHORES DON'T COUNT.)

6. PLAN A DINNER, MAKE A GROCERY LIST,
AND PICK OUT THE SUPPLIES AT THE GROCERY STORE.
(NO, YOU DON'T HAVE TO COOK IT JUST YET.)

7. FIGURE OUT WHICH OF YOUR NEIGHBORS
MIGHT BE A VISITOR FROM ANOTHER PLANET.

8. READ A BOOK ABOUT THE HUMAN BODY AND HOW IT WORKS.

9. DO YOUR HOMEWORK WITHOUT BEING REMINDED.

10. LEARN HOW TO SAFELY USE A SHARP KNIFE AND
(IF YOU CAN GET TO THE COUNTRY) BUILD A FIRE OUTSIDE.

ACKNOWLEDGMENTS

This series began as a birthday present for my daughter, Georgia, and her best friend, Wyatt. I owe Wyatt and his mom, Stephanie Kim Simons, my eternal gratitude for their friendship, enthusiasm, and encouragement.

Thanks as always to Suzanne Gluck and Andrea Blatt at WME for their tireless support. Andrea deserves a medal—or maybe a statue built in her honor. For now, I hope this acknowledgment will suffice!

This series would not have been possible without Anne Heltzel at Abrams, who shared my vision from the very beginning, and Hana Nakamura, who brought that vision to life.

And thanks to Michael Buckley, the funniest man on earth and one of the few adults who know how to enjoy life like a 9-year-old.

ABOUT THE AUTHOR

KIRSTEN MILLER is a renowned author of middle-grade and YA fiction. She lives in Brooklyn with her precocious 10-year-old, who helped write this book. Find out more at kirstenmillerbooks.com.

DON'T MISS

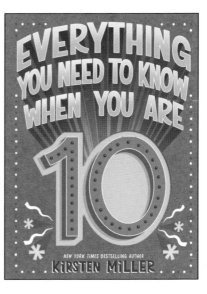

FOR ALL THE BEST SECRETS ABOUT TURNING 8 AND 10!